108 Self-Love Rituals

Michelle Jeovanny Lopez

Title ID: **6022044**
ISBN-13: **978-0692628072**

DEDICATION

To my future daughter, Maileh Jean, may you always remember how deeply loved you are. Thank you for teaching me to believe in the power of the invisible realm. May you dance with the world but always remember the world will adjust to your own self worth.

To Vera and Zella, may you keep dancing and enamoring the world with your fun loving ways. Thank you for reminding me to love myself.

And to all the little girls of the world, old and young, may we forever be reminded of how our inner beauty, love, and light is the soil of the Earth. May the world be your playground to create all the wonders of your soul.

Your love is the light of this word!

THANK YOU'S

With love and gratitude, I bow to you Joydev…
thank you for always believing in me.

To my circle of trust, you know who you are, thank you for always
championing me and being the reflection of
love, acceptance and joy in my life.

To Mom, Jackie O, Jeremy and Melli.. thank you for being my teachers.

Last but not least to Mi Abuelita Querida, Luz Maria.. thank you for being
my lantern in the dark… your love illuminates my darkest hours.

I love you!

Remember God so much that you are forgotten.
Let the caller and the called disappear; be lost in the Call.

RUMI -"Love is a Stranger", Kabir Helminski

MY MUSE

The inspiration for this book came from a thought or better said, a question, that lead to some powerful conversations with friends.

What is love?
What does love look like?
What does love feel like?

I started searching in my own life what generated or caused the feeling of love within me.
What did I love to do? How did I appreciate and love myself? Really. I started thinking what if girls knew the power of self-love.

Learning to love myself through acts of self-love was profound for me. When I applied this concept of self-love rituals with my coaching clients and friends, people began sharing the same experiences.

Loving ourselves felt beautiful, like nourishing the quench of an endless thirst to feel worthy, to feel beautiful, to feel loved. We rejoiced and celebrated in our wholeness.

Self-Love is water to our soil, air to lungs, music to our soul...

108 Self-Love Rituals

Self-love is a practice rarely acknowledged, and seldom discussed. I truly believe it is not spoken about enough. Not long ago there was a quote on social media that went viral, that said, "An act of self-love is a spiritual rebellious act in a world that profits from low self-esteem."

Yet, this one topic, that is clearly very crucial to how we live our lives is generally taboo to most people around the world. It's become a topic uncomfortable to speak about much as politics, religion and extraterrestrials.

Go ahead, and try it. Ask someone randomly, "What did you do for yourself today out of self-love?"

You will, more than likely, get *the deer in headlights expression*, a blank face and shrugged shoulders that answers back with the question, "What are you talking about?" We rarely, if ever, ask ourselves, or each other, how we practiced self-love today.

How <u>did</u> we love ourselves today in a tangible way?

Growing up, that was one of my mother's favorite recitals. She would repeat over and over, "You have to love yourself more." And, my impatience would grow deeper, sometimes to the point of dashing right back confused, "How don't I love myself? How can someone not love themselves?" I would reply.

Over the years I've seen it not only within myself but everyone around me.

A false.. pretentious.. superficial.. lying.. conditional.. hasty... lazy... jealous... unconscious.. momentary... weak.. inactive.. self-defeating... martyred... arrogant.. cheating... kind of love.

I see it in the person who says she loves herself, and, yet allows others to treat her poorly. I see it in the mom or dad who always leaves his or herself for last, exhausted and depleted. I see it in the grandmother who has isolated herself from the world. I see it in the husband desperately holding on to the past. I see it in the college student looking for love in all the wrong places. I see it in the young girl being bullied because she looks different. I see it in the child rebelling against his family.

I remember coaching someone, after listening to them go on and on about how all they truly wanted was a "committed, loving relationship."

So I asked him a question:
"How will you be the source of self-love today?"

In a society programmed to have us focus on our faults, on our flaws and imperfections, on what's not working, on what is lacking or missing in our lives, on what's not good enough, it's become the norm to look outside of ourselves for solutions, answers and *quick fixes* that will alter the way we feel about ourselves.

We have become fixed on the idea of looking outside of ourselves, everywhere else, for that little bit of love and care that might boost our self-esteem, and our day-to-day experience of ourselves.

In this book, we will go over 108 Self-Love Rituals to get you started in completely revamping your life from the inside out. We will discuss in depth how self-love is the root of your success.

You will learn practical steps and ancient rituals to bring alive the love, passion and joy that lives inside of you, while learning how to sustain that fire that burns within us all. You will understand how to harness, nourish and cultivate your energy field with these simple, practical, everyday self-love rituals.

Perhaps your vice is shopping, or, maybe it's working tirelessly on your goals until you exhaust yourself. It could be you are the kind of person who continuously gives to others. You give and give and give until you have exhausted yourself, only to feel burned out in the end.

Maybe you are the one who leaves yourself for last, because you somehow cannot get everything done and still have enough time left to care for your own needs. Trust me, we've all been there once or twice, or, maybe way too often for our own good.

Perhaps self-love is a foreign language we know nothing about, or a subject we know well but are looking to try different rituals. Here's your chance to fully explore *108 Self-Love Rituals* that will dive deep igniting and radiating your true inner self with everything you do.

True love begins with self-love...

We can only offer others that which we have to offer. If we are feeling a certain way about ourselves, it's through that lens that the World will begin to view us.. And, that will mean our relationships with friends to lovers, family and colleagues, even our associations with objects such as goals, business, money, health can be altered through our self-love lens for the world.

Think about it. When we feel great about ourselves we tend to attract even more great feelings and events.

We somehow attract people and happenings that match the energy that we are projecting through our own self-love lens. When we are down about life, the truth is that we are not happy with ourselves. There is something being reflected back to us that heightens our inner discontentment and beliefs about ourselves.

The Harsh Reality

In our lives, fortunately or unfortunately, however we choose to view it, we are the common denominator to everything and all of it. From the relationships to the sacred spaces of home, family, work and community that we have notched into our lives. All of it, everything and everyone you can think of, the common denominator is YOU (ME).

The world responds to how you view yourself, how you treat yourself. Life is simply interacting with how much or how little you value yourself. We receive what we think we can get. We settle for what we believe we can have. Has your self-love become conditional?

The world is simply a reflection, a continuous response to how much or how little you love yourself.

The invitation for the next few days is to observe your thoughts, your action, your intake, your posture.

How we think, what we say and do, how we nourish our mind, body and soul, how we stand and speak, is continuously informing the world who we are, and what we think we are worth.

Love yourself like never before and do it through action, the exact same way you would want *that special one* to treat you.

Love yourself to the point that your aura and energy reject anything and anyone that doesn't know your worth.

Life will adjust to your self-worth.

Believing in yourself is intrinsically tied to how much you value yourself and what you are willing to request the Universe for, loving yourself through tangible acts of love will ultimately set the bar to even your own standards.

In essence, your standards are cultivating through you being your values regardless of what you say, ultimately, it's all up to your congruency. Otherwise, if you are not BEING your values, your vision, if you are not being whatever it is that you say you are seeking, it all becomes empty promises and hollow stands, designed to have you feeling powerless and unworthy.

You are powerful, beautiful and divine.

There is no one out there that can fulfill your purpose and reason for being here.

Trust in that person in the mirror. That person is the rarest commodity of them all! You have something special and unique about you..

It's time to let that person shine like never before. I see you. I believe in you.

Let's begin.

108 Self-Love Rituals

1. Self Love Affirmations:

The power of our thought and spoken word has received so much attention from experts in the field of psychology, transformation and traditional science.

The late Japanese scientist, Masaru Emoto, demonstrated how much power our thoughts, words and conversations have over our bodies, our emotional well being, our relationships, and, our communities as a whole. If you have not seen this experiment, I invite you to take a couple minutes and watch it here:

https://www.youtube.com/watch?v=tAvzsjcBtx8

<<< The key to this first and most important self-love practice is understanding that it takes 21 days for a new beliefs to sprout in our consciousness. This means that by repeating a thought over a span of 21 days will become a belief. But, it doesn't stop there. In order for this new belief to be embedded within your subconscious thought, it will take 40 days of repeating it over and over. >>>

Write down 2 or 3 positive new thoughts that are completely outside the normal thoughts you have about yourself.

For example, if you are shy, new thoughts could be:

"I am a beautiful powerhouse who expresses herself with confidence, grace and love."

If you are feeling a certain way about your body:

"I love my body, my body is a perfect unique treasure that is forever expressing itself with grace, beauty and love."

If you are feeling 'less than' in any particular area whether it's in business, intimacy, or family:

"I am enough. I am more than enough. I am attracting to myself all that radiates true abundance, love and prosperity."

These thoughts are entirely up to you.. designed by you to cultivate and raise the level of positive v bration you are both radiating, and attracting to yourself. Repeating these thoughts over and over will create a new foundation for your self-love.

Post these thoughts in a few different places where you can see them everyday. Bathroom mirrors, nightstands, refrigerators are great places. Place reminders on your phone that will pop up and prompt you to recite your new self-love beliefs.

Trust yourself, and repeat these new thoughts, these affirmations as often as you like. There was a time in my life that I repeated, like a broken record, ore of my own affirmations.

I repeated it so many times that after 3 months a complete stranger was describing me with the exact words I had chosen without his knowledge. No coincidences, right?

Fun Fact: Our brains vibrate at around 75 MHz. . imagine how these new affirmations will begin to raise the vibrations of your thoughts.

2. The Mirror Trick

Speaking to yourself in the mirror has a powerful effect very much like reading your own handwriting. It has been proven scientifically to have such an impact on ourselves and our results.

This self-love practice can go either of two ways. It may be so difficult and painful that tears start welling up as you perform this ritual. Or, it may be such a regenerative and invigorating experience that it will have you hooked. Don't worry about the results!

Accept the feelings and emotions that emerge within you.

The steps are simple but require pure presence and a '*fake it till you make it*' mindset should you experience resistance creeping in.

Say it loud or say it softly.

The key will be to say it with <u>love and conviction</u>, as if the person in the mirror is the most important person in your life, and, that somehow these words are exactly what this person needs to hear in this precise moment.

<u>First Step:</u> Stand about 1 hand's width away from the mirror fully engaging and connecting with your eyes in the mirror.

<u>Second Step:</u> Look straight into your eyes engaging with your pupils for about 10 seconds.

<u>Third Step:</u> Looking straight into your eyes, repeat these words fully connected to your eyes in the mirror as if your spirit and it's projection are one.

"I love you, <your name>.
I really truly love you. Thank you for being you.
Thank you for loving me as I love you.
I love you <your name>. I really truly love you."

I strongly recommend you do this either before or after showering, before or after brushing your teeth or right before going to sleep.

Again, the timing is up to you. What I'm really stressing here is the presence that goes into this exercise. Do it with purpose and conviction.

Bonus: Write about your experience with this specific self-love ritual. How did it feel? Did it feel real? What will it take to feel real and authentic?

3. Take a 5Rhythms Class

Shifting and balancing our emotions requires << MOVEMENT. >> Engaging with our thoughts, in a way that our bodies can fully incorporate these new self-love thoughts, is the key.

Movement creates the kind of clearing that will serve to shift and align our bodies with our new self-love perspectives.

Some people waste valuable time hoping and wishing for a different result, but they never take the time out to clear and move through these spaces of self-confinement with purpose and vigor. We live in a trap that somehow says, "Keep visualizing, and staying positive, and everything will fall into place."

The biggest taboo that we rarely hear about is how movement, or energy in motion, supports us in transcending our self-perceived limitations.

Think about it in these terms, a dusty old room will never be cleaned by you looking at it, or thinking happy thoughts about it. You get to grab that broom, mop and dustpan, roll up your sleeves and clean away.

It's through movement that we can actually start clearing out all that old debris, making space for new, fresh thoughts to emerge.

Call it a reintegration is you will.

"Why 5Rhythms," you might ask?

I had a student once describe human beings as walking universes. I could not help myself. Right away I asked him, "Why?" And, he said, "Because we're just a song in the making, a song that combines everything we think, perceive, believe in, and do into one beautiful verse." The brilliance to know this at such a young age had me in awe of this young leader.

For me personally, 5Rhythms is a life changer. There is no other dance meditation that will have you move like this one and experience wholeness as this class. Below are some quotes from the founder that articulates perfectly this unique and popular dance meditation. Also, check out their website: www.5Rhythms.com

"Waves move in patterns. Patterns move in rhythms. A human being is just that —energy, waves, patterns, rhythms. Nothing more. Nothing less. A dance.

5Rhythms is a dynamic movement practice—a practice of being in your body—that ignites creativity, connection, and community.

5Rhythms transcends dance—movement is the medicine, the meditation and the metaphor. Together we peel back layers, lay our masks down, and dance till we disappear.

While a seemingly simple process, the 5Rhythms practice facilitates deep and unending explorations, moving the dancer beyond self-imposed limitations and isolation into new depths of creativity and connection."

-Gabrielle Roth, Creator of 5Rhythms

Take a 5Rhythms class by yourself the first time, and then, with friends thereafter if you choose.

BONUS: As you move through the class, recite your affirmations. Repeat them over and over feeling the vibrations of the words through your body.

4. Vision Walk

Take a 30min walk by yourself. Focus on your breathing. Bring to mind visuals of your ideal life at a 10.

As you walk, with your mind, take 30 minutes and go down pictures of each ideal life within each domain, your ideal family, ideal relationship, finances, health, work, etc.

Bring to life these ideal scenarios through the out-picturing of your mind as you consciously breathe in and breathe out each visual through your vision walk.

Walking begins to send out neuro sparks down through your body. Your breathing creates a conscious flow that allows you to tap into a higher dimension that begins vibrating through your vision walk.
Trust the flow... if things come up, feel them and let them go. Allow the thoughts to pass freely through you.

Then bring your attention back to your breathing. Breathe life into your visual mind, bring back your attention to consciously visualizing your ideal life scenarios, feeling each scenario through each breath. Walk, breathe, and visualize.

If your attention keeps getting distracted, bring it back to your breathing and continue walking. As you get present to your breathing and walking, present to each step, each breath, bring to mind the ideal life visuals and feel the sensation of bringing them alive as you breathe and walk, presencing each step and each visual simultaneously.

5. Create a 5 Year Bucket List.

Write a list of a minimum of 10 things you will get to create and bring about in the next 5 years. Do you want to go to India for a month and see the ancient temples? Or, is your thing to live in an igloo for a week? Have fun with this one.. make believe 5 years is all you have left, but the irony is that you have a magic wand. The sky's the limit!

What do you wish to do, say, create, experience, feel? What matters most? What would your 5-year Bucket List consist of?

20

6. Letter to my future self.

Quantum physics affirms that we live in a multidimensional reality, and there really is no ineal timeframe as all realities are playing out within this very same moment.

In essence, there's infinite realities taking place right now, and, is possible that our future selves are connected to us just as our past selves are.

Writing a letter to your future self will set in motion a vibration of connection with your higher, wiser self that can provide solutions, guidance and divine interceptions. I know it sounds woo-woo, I get it all the time. But the results are beautiful. The experience feels loving, healing, enchanting; magical, I dare say.

Try it! What do you have to lose anyway?

This ritual is super easy. Write a letter to your future self, whether it's 5, 10, 15, 20, 50 years ahead is up to you. Start with acknowledging yourself for who you are and everything you've accomplished so far.

Bring to light your current situation and ask for specific guidance, healing, support in your desired goals. Thank your future self for listening and for their support.

Save the letter in a private place you won't see it. A great place is hidden within your altar if you have one, under a mattress, in a bank safe, and so on.

7. An Altar.

Creating an altar is HUGE! An altar for many spiritual seekers represents the living embodiment of their temple. We've all heard the expression "mind, body and soul." Right?

The altar is a physical representation of all three in one. A mirror of your house of spirits. The physical representation of the mind.

On the altar you can have people that most inspire you, your image of God(s), endearing letters and above all, pictures of yourself, and/or family and friends, anything that inspires, creates and generates the experience of love.

8. Flowers

Buy yourself a dozen of your favorite flowers and place them somewhere special, either next to your bed, on your coffee table... if you don't have a preference go for red roses.

Why red roses? Roses in particular are known for brightening up the space, raising the vibration of any room. Red is the color of love.
Red roses create a vibration of abundance and harmony. We can see this on a global scale given that we bring flowers to the sick or a new birth, to church, or for altars.

Roses create a vortex that cleanses the space, removing negativity, hurt or anger in any environment.

Other flowers are significant:

- *Carnations* carry a vibration of healing, used for emotional and mental stability.
- *Gardenias* carry a vibration of cooling, clearing and cleansing, absorbing discords.
- *Easter Lily's* heal discordances in sexuality or spirituality.
- *Yellow Star Tulip* develops empathy, allowing to listen and perceive where others are coming from.

9. Hug a Tree

In a recently published book, **Blinded by Science**, the author, Matthew Silverstone, proves scientifically --actually using hundreds of scientific studies that prove trees do, in fact, improve many health issues such as concentration levels, reaction times, depression, stress, headaches and other various forms of mental illness such as ADHD.

Trees carry a very grounded healing vibration when you allow yourself to either hug or sit at the trunk while you close your eyes and morphe vibrationally, become one with your experience.

It has been proven that if you drink a glass of water that has been treated with a 100MHz vibration your blood coagulation rates will change immediately on ingesting the treated water. It's the same with trees. When touching a tree, its different vibrational pattern will affect various biological behaviors within your body.

Hug a tree for at least 5 minutes, but challenge yourself for 10-15min or even 30 minutes. Bring a journal and/or music to give you freedom in the time being next to a tree for extended periods of time if needed.

Bonus: Holds hands with someone you love.

10. Favorite Movie

Watch your favorite movie. Take time for yourself. Have fun with it. Make popcorn or get whatever treats you prefer. What do you love about this movie? What do you love about a particular character in this movie? What challenges can you relate to?

Become absorbed in the experience knowing this movie will always remind you of life's ordinary and dynamic moments merely by watching this movie right now.

Bonus: Watch it with someone special.

11. Earthing

We spend most of our lives walking in sneakers or shoes, and, the infrequent time that we are barefooted, we're usually walking on hardwood floor or some type of tile. Rarely are we, as our ancestors were, roaming over the earth barefoot, connected to the earth.

Earthing similar to tree hugging in the sense that your bare feet are touching the ground, preferably soil or grass. Whatever sitting or standing position you are in, your feet are always touching the ground. Walk on the ground and sit with your feet on the ground.

Do this for about 15-20 min.. even 5 minutes count. It's up to you, but the longer you invest in your self-love ritual, the more benefit you will reap. Your bare feet serve as connectors, thus earthing implies cleansing, restoring, regenerating, stimulating, as we morphe our energetic field with the earth's solid and fertile grounds.

Bonus: Do it with someone special.

12. Self Acknowledgement Letter

Here's an opportunity to finally thank yourself, thank your body, thank your health, your eyes, your courage.

When was the last time you acknowledged yourself?

Writing makes it that much more tangible and material to see these words of acknowledgement through your own writing. Write at least a 2-3 paragraph letter self acknowledging yourself. Make it your best one yet.

Bonus: if you have a friend, have them do one as well. Share what you both got from writing the letter.

13. Gratitude

Write 40 things you are grateful for. Gratitude is the most powerful and highest form of prayer. It carries the vibration of abundance and oneness. Love is experienced when you tap into gratitude. I strongly urge you to create a daily practice of gratitude in either your morning or nightly routine. Creating a daily practice of gratitude will cultivate a vibration of love and abundance.

Right when you wake up or right before going to sleep, write 5-10 things you are grateful for today. In this very moment, what are you grateful for?

Doing this before you sleep allows you to fall asleep in the energy of abundance and gratitude, which is a vibration of expansion and ascension.

Bonus: Do this EVERYDAY, and, share it with one person each day.

14. Love in Action Date – Volunteer

Schedule a 'Love in Action' date. Service is love in action. Each one of us was brought here to earth to make a difference. Make that difference by volunteering.

This is an opportunity for you to turn your focus outward toward the needs of others who have been less fortunate than you. Giving love is the best way to experience it.

Paying your blessings forward creates harmony, abundance and love. Being *in service* to others amplifies the vibration of love within us, as our very essence is simply reflecting back to us a conglomerate of cells and organs in service to one another.

Bonus: Do it with a friend.

15. Love Letter

Write yourself a love letter as if you are your own soulmate... your ideal partner loving you. Write a love letter to yourself expressing that 'once in a lifetime' love, awe, and appreciation for who you are. Pour your heart and soul into this one.

Save this letter in your nightstand or somewhere where you will be easily reminded of all the love swirling inside of you.

16. Massage

Massage has dated back well over 5000 years in the ancient civilizations of China, Japan, India, Egypt, Greece and the Roman Empire, among others. There are so many benefits to receiving a massage; you might want to do some research of your own. But, here's one of the reasons that stands out: Getting a massage is about You being pampered; allowing someone to use their hands to rub, clear and align your energy field.

The touching component alone will give you the human connection that we all yearn for, to some degree, at our soul level. So, go ahead and book yourself a massage. Allow yourself to be pampered through this experience. You deserve it.

17. A Nice Warm Love-Tub

Hot baths also date back thousands of years. When I think of hot baths, I think of the Roman Baths Complex. Roman baths were a part of everyday life in ancient Rome. It gave people a place to cleanse, reflect, mingle and gossip. But, here we are, in modern times, where finding the peace and quiet, or even the time, to prepare a hot tub and soak is seemingly impossible.

Make the time to reward yourself with a hot bath! Include music and candles; extra bonus for rose petals and rose oil. Bubbles are optional. But epsom salt is a must. Get everything ready and prepare to bath for at least 15 minutes, though 30 minutes is ideal.
Simply soak and allow the water to dissolve any toxic thoughts or any physical, spiritual, or mental stress, allowing the water to cleanse your heart and soul. Breathe and soak :)

18. Give out 8 hugs

We all know hugs are great but we rarely give them or even hold an open stance to receive them. In fact, I now sometimes find myself asking for permission by saying, "I'm a hugger." Science has proven that good hugs increases our oxytocin level. This love drug calms your nervous system, boosting positive emotions. This hormone lowers your blood pressure and your cortisol, and significantly reduces your stress, resulting in better, sounder sleep.

Studies show that couples who hug more are more likely to stay together.

This love hormone will have you feeling connected with a sense of belonging. Neuro-economist Paul Zak, known as "Dr. Love," recommends at least eight hugs a day to be happier and enjoy better relationships. And, by the way, the ideal hug lasts 20 seconds.

Psychotherapist Virginia Satir also famously said, *"We need 4 hugs a day for survival. We need 8 hugs a day for maintenance. We need 12 hugs a day for growth."*

Regular hugs provide the following added benefits:

- Cultivating patience and showing appreciation
- **Stimulating dopamine, the pleasure hormone, and serotonin,** for elevated mood
- Balancing out your nervous system for better parasympathetic balance
- Activating the Solar Plexus Chakra, which stimulates your thymus gland, which may help balance your production of white blood cells.

The reasons for giving hugs are endless. This ritual consists of giving and receiving at least 8 hugs. Try to hold on passed the 7 second mark!

BONUS: KISS SOMEONE SPECIAL.

19. Forgiveness Ritual

This one right here is super powerful. Forgiveness seems like it's about someone else, but it's really about you.

By forgiving someone you open up the possibility of releasing whatever pain you've been holding on to, and most importantly that release is creating space in your life.

This ritual requires honesty, courage and conviction to go all the way to the last step.

First, write a list of names and events that you feel unsettled about. Then, write next to each name what, exactly, you feel about the situation. Finally, declare out loud,

"I forgive (name) and accept everything as meant to be. I am free. I am free."

Repeat that process for each name and event, really absorbing the experience of love, acceptance and letting go; and, really forgiving and releasing energetically.

After you have completed your list, burn it, and, throw the ashes on water symbolizing healing and renewal.

20. Violet Fire Ceremony

Create a fire somewhere safe. If not possible, light a candle instead and use the flame as the focal point.

Look into the fire and see the yellow flame.. the violet flame.

Continue gazing into the fire, breathing consciously and repeat 3 times:

> "I AM the Violet Flame.
> I AM the Violet Flame.
> I AM the Violet Flame."

Repeat as often as you like, as you continue gazing into the fire.

Native Americans made fire ceremonies a regular ritual. It garnered peace and joy and a sense of togetherness.

What are the thoughts that will have you express love to yourself as you look into the flames?

Bonus: Journal your experience of The Violet Flame meditation.

21. Morning Stretch

Wake up and STRETCH! Take 10 minutes to really stretch every corner and piece of you from head to toe. Really indulge and move into each stretch from your neck to your wrists and shoulders to fingers and every part of your back, rolling your head around in opposite directions. Totally flex every muscle you can move in your entire body.

22. Food Nirvana

Purchase or prepare your favorite food. Create a beautiful dinner experience for yourself. Indulge and savor each bite as if it were your last meal.

23. Wash, Cut and Style

Pamper yourself to a date with the hair stylist and reward yourself. How you present yourself is not about vanity so long as it is not about showing off to others. When you look your best you are displaying love for yourself, it's about you loving you.

24. Oils

Oils date back to ancient Greece, used for many different benefits, and for all parts of the body, the hair and even the nose as a scent. We enjoy many kinds of oils, so, we decided to list our favorites and their benefits.

- Bergamot is great for calming and soothing, frequently used in massages.
- Clary Sage is used for menstrual cycles, for lifting and lightening the mood.
- Clove is great for teeth and is a powerful antioxidant.
- Eucalyptus is great for the skin, promoting vitality.
- Frankincense is a powerful one for cellular regeneration, promoting relaxation.
- Geranium is perfect for calming the nervous system, and also repels insects.
- Myrrh is great for cleansing mouth and throat, for youthful skin, and emotional balance.
- Patchouli is great for balancing emotions, promotes glowing complexion.
- Lavender is our favorite, releasing tension, relaxing, calming, soothing for sleep.
- Lemon uplifts and aids digestion.
- Lemongrass is great for skins and nails, as well as healthy digestion.
- Peppermint is used for respiratory problems, stomach upsets, and in oral products.
- Sandalwood is great for meditation and skin care, as well as enhancing mood.
- Ylang Ylang is another favorite, great for enhancing and uplifting mood.
- Rosemary, considered sacred by ancient civilizations, for healthy digestion as well as respiratory function and balance.

25. Music - Dance to Your Favorite Song

The best way to clear any negativity, feelings of self-doubt or being stuck is by moving through your emotions. And, there's no better way to do that than to dance and really move through this space and energy. So choose your favorite dance song, closing the door if you have to, and DANCE, DANCE, DANCE your heart away!

26. Morning Pages - Write 3 pages each morning

Julia Cameron created something so beautiful called morning pages. Write 3 pages in the morning, consider it outflowing and clearing your day. Write anything. Just write. And let it go. Whatever you write will be perfect. This ritual is about clearing the energy of the day, clearing any blocks that might hinder or limit your self-expression. It's about clearing the space for your day to take place. Access your creativity, your inner artist.

27. Money Date - Write your actual and ideal budget/savings plan

Money is one energy source some find more of a challenge than others. In use it represents an exchange of energy. And, it begins with us and our beliefs about money.

Our money is also directly tied into our feelings of self worth. It becomes a material extension of us, and, too often, monetizing the value of what we think we are worth.

On one side of a piece of paper write your actual finances, what you owe and what your income is. Get clear on your current financial picture as accurately as possible.

On the other side of that piece of paper write your ideal finances six months from now and one year from now.

Get a blank check or draw one on a piece of paper and write an amount dated 5 years from now. Sign it to the Universe and endorse it to yourself. Put it all away together and place it somewhere you won't really see it.

28. Freedom

Freedom is the ultimate longing that resides within our souls. We crave it because we are it. This self-love ritual is about getting really clear about what freedom means to you. Compose two pages about what Freedom means to you. What does it look, feel, and taste like? What does it really mean to be free? Totally dive into the experience of freedom.

29. Sun Salutations & A Great Workout - Heart Openers & Yoga

However you do your cardio, maybe it's a spinning class for you, a yoga class or a simple total body workout, the point is to strengthen your core and sweat a little :)

The stronger you get, the better you become as a host with a stronger energy field. Look up the sequence of a sun salutation and commit to doing at least 5 sun salutations to get you warmed up before attempting a great workout. Research different heart openers and incorporate them into your workout.

We know spirituality sometimes can be perceived as a negating of the body, declaring we are not our bodies, but, rather our bodies are our temple, as temporary as they are. After all, they do carry us, in our material form, through this lifetime.

Working out is amazing for the body, and for our emotional well being as well. Choose a quick workout, minimum 25 minutes, and show your body love through action.

30. Church / Temple / Gathering

Connect to whatever higher power you believe in, even if you don't believe in God. Honoring what you believe in within a community setting is powerful, regenerating and healing.

Wherever there are two or more gathered in one belief there is power.

Choose a place that resonates with what you believe in. If you don't know of one, now would be a great time to research and try something new.

Visit this sacred place and allow yourself to be inspired by a community sharing their love and vision for their Beloved.

31. The One Gallon Challenge

For 24 hours challenge yourself to drink one gallon of water. If you start to feel sick then stop the challenge.

The goal is to challenge yourself in a fun way, looking at this challenge as a quick detox, and, at the same time, nourishing your body.

32. Mani & Pedi Date

Take yourself on a manicure and pedicure date. Allow yourself to be pampered. Choose your favorite colors. Your hands and feet are extensions, like branches or antennas that send and receive, that touch and feel. Your feet carry your temple, grounding your energy with that soil your feet touch. Love yourself and tune into this simple ritual of pampering yourself.

Bonus: Turn off your cell phone while you're doing it and get a 15 min back or leg rub.

33. Movie Date

Go on a movie date with yourself. If the idea of going to the movie alone seems too weird for you, then invite a friend or significant other. However, I challenge you to go by yourself, <u>especially</u> if it seems weird.

The intention is to be in the experience of going to the movies with yourself, your real soulmate, loving yourself as you would want to be loved through action.

34. Promise Ring

It doesn't have to be a ring. It could be a bracelet, a necklace, something to symbolize the promise to love yourself. This object is worn as a promise to never allow your happiness to depend on anything external other than you. This is the promise to love and accept yourself, no matter what happens, just the way you are, and, just the way you're not.

35. Read a Great Book & Get Lost in It

Reading is a way to open up and expand your imagination. Storytelling with your own voice plays a huge role in speaking to yourself in a new and different way.

The whole purpose is to try new things, if your inner voice is already dreading reading a book. If you love to read then open up a book that makes you wonder, and get lost in the beauty of the story. Here is a list of a few of my favorites.

Great Fiction Reads:
The Alchemist, The Screaming Hawk part 1 and Part 2 The Screaming Hawk Returns, The Palace of Illusions, The Forty Rules of Love, The Disappearance of The Universe, The Witch of the Portobello

Personal Development GREAT Reads:
The Four Agreements, Conversation with God, A New Earth, The Power of Now, Radical Forgiveness, The Five Love Languages, The Fifth Agreement, The Mastery of Love, Ask and It is Given

36. PRAY

As we stated earlier, whatever you believe in, or don't believe in, is not the point. Praying is simply a sacred tool to communicate with ALL there is; with the Universe, with our bodies, with our higher minds, with our hearts, with our soulmates, with our Creator, if that is what you believe in.

It is a tool for speaking into existence that which we believe in, that which we bring alive through our faith,

and through our prayers. Speaking and believing in our words of gratitude and love, through declarations that begin to take form through our action.
First there was the word, and the word was God, like forever highlighting the power of speaking into existence. Our prayers reflecting back to us our beliefs.

We only pray for what we think we deserve, or, for what may seem possible in our realm of possibilities.

But, what if I told you to use prayer like a magic wand, blessing what you have, blessing yourself and all your loved ones, blessing your community and world?

Pray for your fondest dreams.
Bless everything & everyone you speak into.

Use your prayer as your devotion, as your worship. Use your prayer as your magic wand to beautify and enhance, to heal and transcend, to love and forgive.

Use your prayer as your connection to all that is possible and miraculous within you.

37. Zoom into Greatness

Make a list of 40 amazing things about YOU! "What's so great about you?", write it down on paper and frame it or post it somewhere where you can read it often and be reminded of your greatness!

38. Dress UP, SHOW UP!

How you present yourself moment-to-moment is a reflection of who you truly are. Dressing up once in awhile is a great way to boost your energy and mood.

Give yourself the opportunity to clean the mirror (figuratively speaking) and remind yourself of what it feels like to dress up and take your time in dressing yourself up with love, care and attention; really paying attention to the details.

Knock yourself out and allow yourself to shine like never before. You know your 10 like no one else. Be that 10 you want your soulmate to reflect back to you.

39. The Happiness Checklist

Write down 5 to 10 things that make you happy. It could be things you simply like to do, or to possess, or someone you enjoy being around.

What are the things that make you smile? Write them down and save your list for one of those *'just in case days'*.

40. Twin Flame / Soulmate Meditation

Write a letter to your twin flame. Regardless of whether you are with someone or no;, write a minimum one-page letter addressed 'To My Twin Flame or Soulmate,' expressing your love, appreciation, connection, and, admiration; all that you love about your soulmate.

How do you feel when you think of that special someone? And, if you are not with someone describe your relationship in detail. Be specific as to who this object of your affection is,, just who is this lover of yours that's coming your way? Who are they on a soul level?

41. Give out 4 Compliments to Strangers

Use the world as a mirror. By that I mean everything is a reflection of you so go ahead and compliment 4 strangers today and watch how your day is infused with love.

Spread love today and make people feel good about being noticed. You know how it feels to receive a compliment from a stranger.

42. Organize a Space at Home

Organizing is like therapy, it begins to clear the energy and restore its harmony and integrity. Back to our world being our reflection analogy.

Our living spaces are a complete reflection of how we feel, of our mental and emotional state.

Home is an extension of us and a co-creation with the people with whom we live.

There is a great bromide that reminds us, "In the beginning you will find the finish lin.," The integrity of who we are is at the beginning of everything.

Cleaning and organizing a space thoroughly in our home, restoring its integrity brings such power, grace and harmony, but at the source level it heals, clears and creates space within your own electromagnetic field. The experience is very liberating, a deep relief.

The exercise is simply to choose a living space within your home. For example, closets, office space, bathroom, bedroom, living room. Choose one space, clean it, organize it, and, do whatever is needed to bring that space back to a **10** if not a **12** :)

If you are one of those *neat-freaks* who "has a place for everything, and, everything in its place" then look into your life at what areas need to be shuffled around, shifting the energy of the space around.

Choose one space and rearrange everything so the energy flows in a different direction.

43. Mandala Coloring Meditation

Research mandalas until you find one that stands out for you. Print out a mandala that inspires you and get your coloring markers/crayons out. Color this mandala with much care and love, really paying attention to the details, coloring every space. Use as many colors as you wish, allowing your creativity and imagination to run wild.

Coloring mandalas promotes relaxation, balancing the body's energies, enhancing your creativity, and supporting healing.

Mandalas come from the sanskrit word meaning circle, without beginning or end. These beautiful images carry a healing vibration we bring to life through our colors. These images have been used for ages to bring about healing.
Simply set your intention and allow your colors to invoke the divine powers of this mandala.

44. Thank You Notes

Write 3 *Thank You* notes to people who have made a significant positive impact in your life; people who you rarely ever get a chance to thank and appreciate as much you should. Giving thanks is the highest form of prayer.

When we appreciate what we have, life seems to expand with more of those affirmations. But when we carry it out and give thanks to the people in our lives, we create an opening for love and abundance to be self-expressed.

Take this opportunity to remind the people in your life that you love them, and, that life is extra sweet because of them. This little ritual will have the mirror reflect back to you your very own reminder one day when needed. Trust. Thank the people you love through a good ole' fashioned handwritten letter :)

45. A 24hour Technology Fasting

Yes, that's right, for one day -24hours, you will abstain from the use all forms of modern technology: phone, computer, gadgets, T.V., radio; anything and everything that has a battery even if it's built in, or a plug (unless needed for meal preparation, or an emergency. Give yourself this treat. And, you'll discover 24 hours goes by faster than you think. Set yourself up to win, letting the people you wish know about your technology fasting.

Take one day to really reflect and get clear about what you want to create in this lifetime and why. Reflect on how technology supports your goals. And be honest with yourself if it sometimes serves as a distraction.

Create new declarations for how you get to use technology to best serve your vision.

46. The 'Everyone is Right' Muse

For just one day, make everyone right. Do not argue, debate or negate anything. Everyone is right, regardless of whether you know they are wrong. This exercise is about refraining from expressing and exercising your opinions.

Giving up our need to be right in any situation will affirm your ability to "let someone else be strong."

Some may question, how this is relevant to loving ourselves? Well, if you think about it, love resides where there is harmony.

Wherever there is conflict, however insignificant and harmless it may appear in the moment, wherever there is conflict, there lives only the illusion of love. Again, just for one day, practice this self-love ritual by allowing everyone to be right.

Everyone is right. It doesn't make you less in any way. Although your ego may fight you to say something, because it knows best, just remember, "Everyone **else** is right!" The moment we release our need to be right, we allow love to merge our opinions as one.

47. Favorite Perfume/Cologne

Wear your favorite perfume/cologne and really go lavish with it for this ritual. Allow your scent to enter the room well before you do. Allow yourself to bask in the scent that you love. If you don't have a favorite perfume/cologne, what a great day to go test some new ones and see which scent stands out for you. And voila! There you have it! Now go and wear your favorite scent.

48. Funny Movie or Live Comedy Show

Watch a funny movie or go out in town and catch a live comedy show. If you don't have access to a local comedy show, then watch a comedy show on television or online. Laugh and give yourself permission to really laugh.

Life can sometimes make us super serious and uptight, we forget to laugh and enjoy the journey. Take this opportunity to really laugh your heart and soul off. Bonus if tears of laughter magically appear.

49. Dream Boards & Vision Boards

Yes visuals are the best.. vision boards are notorious for being catalytic in making dreams happen. Vision boards are super powerful. There are any number of leaders and visionaries who stand behind this tool of manifestation.

Create a 5-year vision board. If you have one already, use this opportunity to update it and add a little more love to it. Make this vision board so identifiable with you, that no one will deny that it's yours with just one glance.

Have fun declaring your dreams as you see them within your heart and soul. Be as self-expressed as possible with colors, pictures, words, this is your master piece. This is where your dreams are spawned in art-form.

The beauty of vision boards is that the brain cannot always distinguish between that which is real from what is not, thus setting in motion The Law of Attraction.

Visualizing and cultivating within us the vibration of our desires and dreams through this beautiful, if somewhat self deceptive, self-love ritual is both very powerful, and gratifying! It may even attract those <<vibrations>> into our lives.

Take your time, there's no getting it right, simply have fun experimenting with visuals that bring your vision to life! Don't worry, you will go blind with so much love!

50. Take a New Class

Whether it's a singing class, an acting class, cooking class or learning how to play an instrument, the subject matter of this new class is not as important as getting you out there trying something new, something that perhaps was a once-forgotten passion or fling that may still spark within you.

This self-love ritual is about trusting those sparks, those soft impulses that nudge at the "what ifs." Trust your intuition, and be uninhibited just once. What might you want to try, perhaps even lust after just for fun, and for the sake of something new?

51. Get a Makeover (for Guys:: get a Facial)

Makeup dates back to early Egyptian times recorded around 3500 BC. On a universal note, makeup has been faithful to 3 fundamental principles: It has been used to even the skin tone, to redden the cheeks and lips, and, to darken the eyes, creating a youthful fertile appeal.

It has been recognized across the ages that women are more conducive to sex, and appealing to men when they are in their menstrual cycle. Their cycle is believed to fluster the cheeks, and redden the lips.

Get yourself a makeover today. Go somewhere the makeup artist can create a couple of different looks, perhaps formal and informal.

52. Get a Facial

Facials come in different styles from creams, to oils, scrubs and even mud. Choose one that peaks your interest and have your facial gift by you for you. Enjoy the love!

53. Buy a One Way Ticket

Pick a place from your bucket list and book a one way flight. Congrats for being spontaneous and get ready for a crazy fun adventure!

54. The Complainer Challenge

For 3 days the challenge is not to issue a single complaint. *No complaining for 3 days.* You must do 10 sit ups for any complaint that slips past your lips. The key is to not resist anything that comes up, and, to honor all offers as is accepting everything as it comes.

55. Say YES!

For one day or however you set the time frame, you are to say yes to everything. And, if you refuse to agree to something, you must then say that you would "rather, or prefer, to do this" and offer an alternative. The key is to maintain a "yes" open state of mind, fully engaging with life.

56. Sun Gazing

For minimum 15 to 25 minutes of "sun gazing," facing toward the sun, (caution: Avoid retinal damage. Never look directly at the sun.) this helping activate your pineal gland or third eye energy. Sun gazing is very powerful and needed. Sun exposure is vital to our bodies and well-being. Take some time to be under the sun.

57. Drive to the Beach

Spend a few hours at the beach, but, no less than 45 minutes, if that's all you can spare, to take off your shoes, and walk by the water's edge. Leave your cell phone in the car or turn it off.

Unplug from everything, and, just connect to the water, to the waves, the sand, and the scent of it all. Look into the vastness of the water, how boundless it is.

Many scientists believe that mankind emerged from the sea as did so many amphibian life forms. Water, particularly sea water, is so very much a part of who we are.

Our bodies consist of 75-80% water, which accounts, in part, for why water is such a healing force and connector to our subconscious. I believe the deep, still, blue water is calling to ours.

Allow yourself to unplug and admire this living phenomenon, that seems to breath with us.

58. Get an Aura Photograph

Take an Aura photograph and enjoy the colors. Have someone fully versed interpret it for you. Understand, and, come to know the beauty in capturing this still shot of your energy and how impermanent such pictures are.

59. Soul Cycling

Soulcycle has completely changed the indoor fitness industry. This highly revered 45 minutes that can change your body and life is the funkiest experience of cycling you will ever have, if you haven't done so already. Take a 45min Soulcycle class either alone, or with a buddy, and, have fun with it.

60. I Forgive Myself Letter

Write a letter forgiving yourself for anything that happened that you regret, and still hold negative energy from. Whatever you're feeling incomplete with, here's your chance to really clear the space and convert that energy into a "rebirth." After you finish your letter, burn it. Allow the smoke to release you from any guilt or shame.

As the smoke rises repeat *"I am free"* at least 3 times... You are free now.

61. Intentions Setting

Write down 5 Intentions for this year. State your goals, yes, and, the intention behind each goal. Set your intentions and place them somewhere where you will be reminded of the essence of your intentions.

62. Your Will

Compose your will right now, making crystal clear how you would like to see events unfold if something were to take your life, or incapacitate you.

Take at least 15min to assess how you would like your affairs to be handled. Put it all in writing and save it. Bonus points if you take the matter all the way and document your will legally.

63. Closet Makeover

Dedicate at least 30 to 45 minutes to this activity. Doing a closet makeover requires focus, clarity and purpose. What are the things that you have outgrown? What items are just not your style anymore? Which items are broken?
Clear out space intentionally. Determine a minimum number of items to be cleared out, perhaps 10 pieces, before commencing the work.

64. Power Stance

"You are very powerful, provided you know how powerful you are." ~Yogi Bhajan

How powerful are you? This ritual is all about your declaring into existence your power and purpose. Write 3 pages on your power.

Declare the who, what, when, how, describing your power. Dig deep. What is so powerful about you?

Remember, the fact that there is no one out there exactly like you, is the essence of your power!

65. Underwear Upgrade

Take an hour to fully indulge in buying new undies. Take the time to really find the underwear that you love, and, that flatters your body. An underwear upgrade is so needed sometimes. Go ahead and splurge on yourself a bit. Have fun!

66. Change Your Bed

This ritual is simply involves upgrading your bed covers and look. Get some funky decorative comfy pillows. Invest in a new and different bedspread. Get new head pillows and blankets. Select different colors, patterns, and texture.

The idea is to completely revamp your bed, the place you spend quite a bit of your time. Do some research, if needed, to get interesting, and appealing styles and themes. Then order the ones that you absolutely fall in love with.

67. Be the Poem

Create a poem for yourself, dedicated to you. A beautiful quote: "If you can't be the poet, be the poem." Shower yourself with love through a beautiful poem created by you.

68. Photo Collages

Create two different collages. Research online to get different visuals of styles, preferences, themes, and colors adopting and composing one for yourself, and one for someone else. Have fun creating memories that will surely have an impact for years to come.

69. Star Gazing

Take time to look up at the sky. If that's not possible then watch some videos online. See what the stars reflect back to you. Star gazing is a perfect opportunity for prayer and intention settings. Invest at least 15min in Star Gazing and getting lost in the stars, literally.

70. Crystals – Rose Quartz

Buy yourself a rose quartz and wear it for at least 15min. Lay down and place it on your heart and allow it to clear the energy over your heart.

Rose quartz is considered the 'Love Stone,' the unconditional love energy that the rose quartz emanates is perfect for opening the heart chakra. It's used to invoke and heal love in all areas from self, intimacy, family, work, etc. The Rose quartz is used to raise self-esteem and a strong sense of self-worth.

71. Spin in Circles

Rotate at least 3 to 5 times in circles. Set your inner child free through this simple self-love ritual. As you spin, let go of every thought, every task. Let go of everything and set your heart free with every spin. Put on music if that is supportive :) and have fun with this ritual!

72. Foot Soak

Soak your feet for a minimum of 15 minutes in a hot bucket of one of the following 'do it yourself' Foot Soaks & Scrubs:

- Brown sugar, baking soda and olive oil
- Epsom salt, baking soda, lime and peppermint oil
- Rosemary, peppermint oil and baking soda
- Camphor, eucalyptus and honey
- Coconut oil, epsom salt, baking soda
- Lavender oil, epsom salt, baking soda
- Tea Tree, baking soda, epsom salt, peppermint oil

73. A Self Love Ceremony - Marry Yourself

Create a small sacred ceremony for yourself, pick your love song, write your pledge or vow.

Committing to yourself, honoring, and loving yourself requires an awareness to cultivate that kind of connection with yourself.

It's a daily moment-to-moment practice that demands your time, focus and effort; the type of commitment that trumps feelings, emotions, and even stagnancy and complacency. Reflect and write down the kind of partner you wish to marry.

Reflect on whether or not you carry and demonstrate these values to yourself. It is the honoring of oneself that will open the doors for another to do the same.

Here's an example:

I pledge to wake myself up, never hold back, have nothing to lose, go all the way, kiss the stormy sky, be the hero of my own story, ask for everything I need and give everything I have, take myself to the river when it's time to go to the river, and take myself to the mountaintop when it's time to go to the mountaintop. You may kiss yourself on your own lips. (kiss a mirror if need be)

Make a promise to yourself to love yourself like never before.

74. Professional Photo Shoot

Book a professional photo shoot, bonus points if you make it sensual and sexy. Capture timeless still shots of yourself in your absolute best version of yourself from great attire, makeup, to hair and accessories.

Explore your sensual side through beautiful poses on camera. Learn to settle into your most raw, authentic inner self. Bask in knowing that you are beautiful, powerful, and divine. HAVE FUN WITH THIS ONE!

Bonus: Send yourself flowers to the appointment and have a friend take pictures of the photo shoot in session so you feel like a true celebrity.

75. Champagne & Roses

Get yourself a champagne you love with roses, bonus points if you get chocolate covered strawberries and candles. Make it a date night with yourself, a toast to your dreams, hopes and aspirations. Make it a beautiful evening to remember.

76. Flowers for Someone Special

Buy and send flowers to someone special like mom, dad, grandparents, siblings, friends, co-workers, etc. Send them with a thank you note expressing your love.

77. Bonsai Tree

Buy a bonsai plant, nurture and care for it. Bonsai are a blessing in spaces, nurturing and healing for the space to be fertile.

78. Home

Watch the movie *Home* and reflect on the planet Earth. See all of its beauty and wonder, see what this movie brings to you.

79. Full Moon Water Ritual

Pour 3 cups of water, one each for your past, present, and future. As you drink and pour a little on the ground, announce your intention to restore and heal any parts of your past, present, and future that may need attention and care.

80. Full Moon Fire Ritual

Write on one side of an index card all the things you are letting go of. And, on the other side, write a full moon intention. Burn the index card allowing your fears to dissolve and your intentions to rise through the smoke. Enjoy this sacred ritual.

81. New Moon Ritual

Get a new moon journal and create a ritual out of scheduling new moon dates where you get to write at least one page of what your goals are starting 6 months out.

Make it a memorable event you look forward to. Turning this ritual into a monthly habit pattern will have you outflowing and expressing your dreams, goals and aspirations. What are your mission and purpose? What inspires you?

This monthly affair is a golden opportunity to dream big.

Bonus is you light candles and get flowers.

82. Local Adventure

Write down 5 things in your city that you have never experienced. For example, if you live in New York City and have never visited the Empire State Building or the One World Exhibit. Choose one and go today. Take yourself on a local adventure!

83. Road Trip

Take a minimum 90-minute road trip somewhere you can easily go off to for a day. Learn to just hop on and go, even if you have children. It's important to practice non-attachment and removing yourself far enough from the equation to create space for you to zoom out and observe it from a higher perch.

Road trips are great for clearing the mind and taking time to reassess and reevaluate certain things in life.

Bonus points if you make it a sleepover.

84. Self-Love Meditation

Turn on a Myrrh Incense and sit in lotus position, bringing all your attention to your heart chakra, feeling with each heartbeat a pulse radiating through your heart chakra.

Focus all your attention and visualize a fire burring and expanding within your heart chakra, clearing out all negativity and barriers to love as it keeps radiating and spewing out energy.

This ritual is perfect with candles and incense to invoke self-love and healing, and clearing your heart chakra. Self-love promotes clarity and compassion, a deeper connection, a knowing and appreciation for who you really are.

85. Art Therapy

Create a piece of art, get the markers/crayons/pencils/water colors out and create a personal masterpiece that reflects all your love and creativity.

This artwork is a self-expression of you, capturing a fragment of pure divinity. Trust the magic inside of you. Let go of your need for perfection, and any self doubt, and, finally allow yourself to create freely.

86. Lie in the Grass

Take 15 minutes to lie in the grass. Connect to the beautiful Earth and it's stillness. Feel the authenticity as you lie on her.

87. Your Story

Write 3 pages minimum on your story from birth till now. What's your story? Write your bio, but, emphasize the way you want people to remember you.

Bonus, if you include pictures.

88. Your Why

Create a minimum 45 second video recapping your why. Why do you do what you do? What's your why for getting up every morning and getting things done, for putting up with the crap, for pushing through your self-perceived, and imposed limits?

This video should be as creative, soulful and original as possible. This is for you, by you, where your authenticity serves to remind you why you do the things you do. This video is simply a reminder self-expressing your love and reason for being here, and, for doing the things you do.

Bonus if you get other people on this video.

89. Light Sparklers

Buy some light sparklers and spark them at night. Visualize in action celebrating your dreams. See your dreams really happening. Celebrate your greatness. Celebrate the gift of being alive!

90. Karaoke - Sing Your Heart Out

Go out to a karaoke and sing your heart out. Singing is so good for the soul, it has you break through energy blocks in the throat and has you outflowing your energy. Go out and have some fun! Include friends if it's less awkward.

91. Listen to a Healing Love Vibration - 528Hz (Solfeggio)

Grab your headphones and go on Youtube.com. Research Love healing vibrations of 528 Hz. Choose one that stands out for you, and listen to it either before you sleep or as you are reading or writing.

Listen to the tune as you consciously set the intention to open up your heart and allow the frequency and the vibrations to morphe with your own energy field, healing and releasing all self-imposed blocks and barriers. This is a great way to raise your vibration!

92. Create a Loving Community

Building a loving community that inspires you and uplifts you is so important for your day-to-day experiences. To love and be loved as they say is the name of the game, creating a loving community around you will propel you forward as you will feel that you belong to a community that is a beautiful reflection of who you are, thus motivating you to keep growing and expanding.

93. Integrity List

Create a list of any and all broken agreements you have, or others have made with you. Regardless of who drew up the agreement, if something did not happen, or was left incomplete, unsaid, or unfinished, it created a loss of power. Your energy field becomes weak.

This list should include anything and everything that you feel out of alignment with, anything you gave your word to perform, or anything that you feel someone or some situation has hindered.

After you have completed your list, reflect and assess which ones are real for you still serving your purpose and vision. And, eliminate the ones that are outdated and no longer serve your purpose or vision.

Create a schedule to complete each week certain tasks off of your integrity list. This will start to restore integrity, stemming the loss of power in those areas of your life, and thereby freeing you up to be fully self-expressive in your life. This ritual will give you direct power over your life.

94. The WWFM Radio Transmission

Take a WWFM inventory list of *'What's Working For Me*,' and focus on what is working in your life. Write it all down and really appreciate the things that are working out. Put it on the fridge.

We often get so caught up in what's not working that we forget to appreciate, take stock of, and focus on the things that are good in life. We have so much working out if we'd only open our eyes and take the time to see all the good, all the positive, all the things we take for granted.

Make your WWFM list, and, as you write it down, amplify and broadcast the energy of gratitude.

95. Family Tree

Create a family tree.. one page with pictures of your family and its origins. Next to their names and pictures, write a brief memory that bonds you forever. Place it somewhere meaningful where you can see it often. An altar is a great place for starters.

Bonus: Share this beautiful family piece with someone special.

96. Language

The energy behind your words and thoughts is calibrating at a specific rate, vibrating at a certain frequency. This self love ritual is about consciously choosing our thoughts and words as we elevate our language.

Make a quick 5 word list that you will eliminate to choose the words and phrases that will replace them.

Establish your overall intention from how you want to feel about yourself, and how you want people to feel after speaking with you. How do you want your words to come across on the other side?

Make a conscious effort to attract support from others holding you accountable for your choices in elevating your language.

Bonus: Create some post its to remind you that 'Language creates your reality.'

97. Your Life Plan

Your ability to create clarity for yourself and visualize where you need to be at any particular part of the day will empower you in every moment. Create a *Sunday Self-Love Ritual* to plan your week and month ahead, detailing all the agreements you are committing to honor, thus painting a full picture of how you choose to mold your days and weeks ahead.

Those who invest time to put pen to paper and break down a plan of action ultimately are the ones who create results in their lives. You will thank yourself for this ritual, to love yourself enough to honor the greatest freedom we have, which is the ability to determine the course of our life.

98. Fruits & Veggie Fast

The body is our temple, a loving vessel that carries our soul if not the other way around, where our soul carries our temple from one act to another. This self-love ritual is a challenge in which for one day all you eat and drink is fruit, veggies and water.

The purpose of this fast is to absorb all nutrients and antioxidants found in these fruits and greens. One day won't kill you, but will make you that much stronger. Love your body through this 24-hour challenge.

99. Define Your God

Exploring your spirituality is fundamental, and the basis for real love and faith to take place in your life. The key to loving yourself comes from knowing who you are.

This self-love ritual is about exploring and discovering your spirituality. Write 2 pages on who your God is, regardless of what you believe in, describe what it is that you believe in.

Describe who and where your Creator resides. Who are you and where do you come from? Write as authentic an account as possible as you describe your God. What are your God's qualities, strengths and powers? What's so great about your Creator or Higher Power?

100. Your Happy Place

Close your eyes and visualize your happy place. Bring to mind that place that makes you smile. Maybe for you it's at the beach, an open field, or on a mountaintop. Maybe it's home, a bonfire at night, or a day at the spa.

Picture yourself there, and, really allow the scenes to come alive through your imagination. Feel the happy place brewing inside of you and smile.

Congratulations, you have now created your *happy place*. Go there, and make it a ritual to escape to it throughout your day.

101. Cooking Class & Food Journal

Take a new cooking class.. something that inspires you and seems like fun. Book it and have fun learning to prepare new foods for your temple. Food is such a great healer, great food is like great therapy. It literally takes your mind off of everything.

Bonus: Journal your food intake for 3 days and then reflect upon, and, assess your eating habits.

Set new goals with clarity and the proper structure in place for what you intend your new food intake to be. Celebrate each day as a win as you create the awareness to choose better nutrition for yourself.

102. A Celebration List

Create a list of things to do to celebrate, reward, motivate and incentivize yourself. Keep this list handy for you to celebrate and treat yourself for simply doing your best. Each week make it a ritual to really celebrate yourself.

This will cultivate the energy of self-love, attention and care that our emotional, mental and physical well-being demand of us.

103-A. Sacred Masturbation –
Rated R version for the sexually active folks.

Our sexuality is such a big part of what drives us. How we feel about our sexuality causes us to come across in a certain way, directly affecting our self-expression, our confidence, and our intimacy. This self-love ritual is about letting yourself go and releasing all inhibitions.

Masturbate yourself to the point of climaxing fully. Create the ambience and vibe you need to love yourself to the point of giving yourself an orgasm.

See how sensual you can make this experience for yourself. See how self-expressive you can be as you explore your sexuality and all the things that give you pleasure.

103-B. Sacred Pleasure –
Rated PG for the beloved virgins or nonsexual peeps.

Appreciating our bodies is fundamental to our self-expression. If you are not sexually active, a virgin or celibate by choice (which is a powerful self-love ritual all in itself), for those that have yet to explore their sexuality fully, use this ritual as a way to explore, appreciate and physically love your body through touch.

Take 15 minutes either in the shower or in bed, you can create a sensual vibe for yourself if you want to go all the way, but this ritual is about you sensually touching every part of your body, from your legs to your face.. touch and love every part of you. Consciously send loving thoughts through your fingertips as you caress your body.

104. The Biggest Lessons

Write a letter to your younger self detailing your biggest lesson in life so far. Life means nothing if we are not taking its lessons with us, fully integrating these lessons into our lives. What has been your biggest lesson so far? What did it mean and how have you grown from the experience?

Documenting, and acknowledging these lessons on paper is powerful as it provides the grounds for you to love yourself, learning from your mistakes, honoring these lessons as part of the miracles and blessings within your journey that have helped you grow, expand, and move forward in your life with purpose and power.

105. The Good Morning "I love you" A Morning Self-Love Ritual

Make it a habit to say, "Good morning' to everyone you encounter. And, if you have a family, or live with your significant other or a roommate, practice saying 'I love you' to the people you live with at home. Say "Good morning" to everyone who crosses your path.

Create the habit of wishing people a great day in the morning. This outward self-expression of love will return tenfold. Polish the world's reflection by showering the world in front of you with love and great morning wishes.

106. Quiet Time - Learning to be still and listen

Taking time for simply quieting the mind and keeping still is such a powerful regenerator. Even if it's only for 5 minutes, make time to settle down and be still, really listening to your soul at a deeper level.

This practice will develop a stronger connection to yourself, learning to listen to your body and higher self is an art you master with practice.

107. A Conversation With Your Fears

Write down all your fears and doubts. Write them down and make sure you feel each one as you acknowledge your fears. Thank them for protecting you in their own way. **Tell each fear, "it's okay to let go, I've got this."**

When you finish writing all your fears down, burn the letter and allow all your fears and worries to dissolve into the smoke. See how your love transcends your fears into the smoke.

You are loved beyond your fears and imagination. Through the smoke, feel the love uplift you.

108. Schedule Your Self-Love Rituals, i.e. Schedule a Yoga class, schedule your rituals.

The real mastery behind success is consistency. Scheduling and making your self-love rituals actually occur is vital to building your self-love practice.

It's not what you say that matters, but, more importantly, the extent to which you honor your words with consistent action.

Loving yourself requires action... real tangible action. Take time out each week to get clarify what you will do for yourself, how you will practice self-love, and, how will you love yourself?

Make it real by scheduling your self-love rituals every week and honoring your word as if everything depended on it.

Questions for you to dive in a little deeper:

- What's my very own Self Love Ritual?
- What is the #1 thing I love to do?
- What do I love most about myself?
- Who am I and what is the vision I hold for myse f?
- What's my purpose?
- What's next for me?
- How will I honor and love myself?
- What am I grateful for?
- What does love mean to me and how do I express it?

What is Love after all?

Love is love.. an act... a devoted action, a 4 letter word that creates a feeling, a stand, a connection that bonds us all. But what is love after all? Nothing but a space we create all the meaning we give to this word.

This 4 letter word is used and abused in so many words, being thrown around like a beat up rag, spammed out and completely desensitized. We say it, we think we mean it, but then we fall short of really being it, expressing it, and honoring this 4 letter unifying force that lives within us all.

However you choose to practice your self-love rituals, whichever rituals you choose is entirely up to you.

There is no right or wrong here, there is no 'this way is better,' there is no way of doing it really as each person is different.

You simply have to trust and listen to what your body is calling for.

Listening is an act of self-love, stemming from a desire to be in the receiving mode, listening with openness and eagerness to what the spirit is yearning for.

These 108 Self-Love Rituals are practices meant to be experienced, not memorized as answers that remain a concept.

108 Self-Love Rituals is more than a book. From now on it serves as a compass for you to answer your deepest questions, to reveal your realizations of greatness, to manifest your most magnificent self, to love yourself beyond doubt.

In every moment we have the opportun ty to love. And that love extends to family members, friends, colleagues and even complete strangers.

How you love yourself will ultimately determine how you love and how you show up in the world.

May you experience the divinity and greatness of your soul through these 108 Self-Love Rituals.

MICHELLE JEOVANNY LOPEZ

- ABOUT THE AUTHOR -

Michelle Jeovanny Lopez is a life and business coach, a transformational leader and youth speaker. She is the co-founder of Dignity University, a transformational company that serves to inspire and empower people to realize their full potential. She is a mystic, an author that writes from her heart and calls on her readers to follow their heart and trust their spunk. She loves to travel the world and share her message, inspiring people, both young and old, to follow their true calling.

For more information, please contact the office at:

info@dignityuniversal.com
www.dignity.univeristy

To keep in touch with Michelle Jeovanny and stay up to date with her latest motivational quotes, tips and thoughts:

www.MichelleJeovanny.com
www.Linkedin.in/michellejeovanny
www.twitter.com/michellejeovanny
www.instragram.com/michellejeovanny

www.ingramcontent.com/pod-product-compliance
Lightning Source LLC
LaVergne TN
LVHW010025070426
835509LV00001B/4